Two Elegies of Hope
Pedro Mir

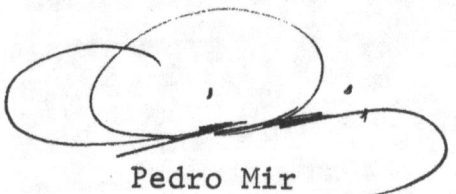
Pedro Mir

Two Elegies of Hope
Pedro Mir

Hurricane Neruda & To Julia with No Tears

Translated by Jonathan Cohen
Foreword by Chiqui Vicioso

Spuyten Duyvil
New York City

Copyright © 1975 by Pedro Mir
Copyright © 1998 by Pedro Mir
Copyright © 2019 by Carmen Mesejo Vda. Mir
Copyright © 2019 by Chiqui Vicioso
Copyright © 2019 by Jonathan Cohen

ISBN 978-1-949966-56-5

In the original publication of *EL HURACÁN NERUDA* by Editora Taller (Santo Domingo, D.R.), Pedro Mir included this note:

Corregido el 8 de septiembre de 1975 y
finalmente (al menos en apariencia) el
2 de noviembre del mismo año
por tercera vez.

[Revised on September 8, 1975, and
finally (at least it seems) on
November 2 of the same year
for the third time.]

Gracias to dear friends Edith Grossman and David Unger for their critical readings of the translations.

Grateful acknowledgment is made to Joseph Schneberg for use of his portrait photograph of Pedro Mir.

Cover portraits by Pedro Abreu, with gratitude.

Library of Congress Cataloging-in-Publication Data

Names: Mir, Pedro, author. | Cohen, Jonathan, 1949 May 4- translator. |
   Vicioso, Sherezada, 1948- writer of foreword. | Mir, Pedro. Poems.
   Selections | Mir, Pedro. Poems. Selections. English
Title: Two elegies of hope : Hurricane Neruda & To Julia with no tears /
   Pedro Mir ; translated by Jonathan Cohen ; foreword by Chiqui Vicioso.
Description: New York City : Spuyten Duyvil, [2019] | Parallel text of
   original poems in Spanish and English translations. |
Identifiers: LCCN 2019037235 | ISBN 9781949966565 (paperback)
Subjects: LCSH: Mir, Pedro--Translations into English.
Classification: LCC PQ7409.M58 A2 2019 | DDC 861/.64--dc23
LC record available at https://lccn.loc.gov/2019037235

Contents

Foreword: Don Pedro Mir and His Hope for the Future   ix

Translator's Preface: Journey into These Poems of Pedro Mir   xiii

El huracán Neruda
Hurricane Neruda

1. Han pasado las horas sobre el volcán Neruda
   A lot of time has passed over Neruda Volcano   5
2. ¿Qué ha sucedido, Padre? Súbitamente nos agravia todo
   What's happened, Father? Suddenly everything disturbs us   7
3. ¿Qué ha sucedido, verdadero Padre del huracán
   What's happened, true Father of the hurricane   9
4. La historia es muy sencilla
   The story is very simple   11
5. La aurora tiene en su falda
   Dawn has a free-spirited band   13
6. Y esto nos explica la situación neruda
   And this explains the neruda situation   17
7. ¡En Chile! ¡No hay un minuto que perder
   In Chile! There isn't a minute to lose   21
8. Y así avanzaron en Chile con esta canción desesperada
   And so they advanced in Chile with this song of despair   25
9. Y cuando ardiendo la fruta se prodiga
   And when the copious fermenting fruit   29
10. Entonces podemos anunciar que hemos entrado estrepitosamente
    Then we can proclaim that we have spectacularly entered   33
11. Y eso es todo. Han pasado las horas y han caído
    And that's all. Much time has gone by and fallen   41
12. Y tú descansa, Padre, que todos los hombres
    And you sleep, Father, as all of us men   45
13. Y [...] para dejar constancia
    And [...] for the record   47

A Julia sin lágrimas
To Julia with No Tears
1. Por un camino de sal que tiene el sol
   By a road of salt that belongs to the sun — 53
2. Y tal fue la voz que alimentaba el eco y tal
   And hers was the voice that fed the echo and so — 57
3. Por un camino que tiene el sol
   By a road that belongs to the sun — 59
4. Porque la Cuestión de Santo Domingo
   Because the Question of Santo Domingo — 63
5. Pero ¿por qué me la hicieron salir
   But why did they make her leave naked — 67
6. Ahora no venga nadie a la Quinta Avenida
   Don't anyone come now to Fifth Avenue — 69
7. Ciertamente a Julia de Burgos
   Of course to Julia de Burgos — 73
8. Por el estricto rostro de las avellanas
   By the strict face of filberts — 75
9. Vendrán los días y las melodías
   Days and melodies will come — 77
10. Vendrán las mariposas de las factorías
    Butterflies will come from factories — 79

About Cohen and Vicioso — 81

FOREWORD:

DON PEDRO MIR
AND HIS HOPE FOR THE FUTURE

The national poet of the Dominican Republic, Don Pedro Mir, was a survivor of multiple sorrows. Since he was a boy, from the absence of his mother; then later, as a young man, from the persecution of Trujillo's dictatorship, which forced him to go into exile.

Don Pedro is an oceanic poet whose work can only be compared to Walt Whitman's, in its symbolic range, for its movement between the allegorical and the biographical and between the biographical and the historical, for its course through the geography and traditions of the peoples to whom he sings. With one big difference: Walt was the poet of the North American man and woman, in the singular, and Don Pedro was a poet of the multitudes of Pan America.

"Hurricane Neruda" is a song-lament for Salvador Allende, through the hurricane force of Pablo Neruda. It is an elegy in which Don Pedro shows his deep knowledge of the double tradition of the Hispanic lyric, and especially in particular the work of Federico García Lorca, and his "Lament for Ignacio Sánchez Mejías."

It has the same poetic construction, with verses that are repeated as in a litany, the kind sung at funerals and at holy hours in homes in the Caribbean; it has the same musicality, verses and verses that repeat themselves in a growing wave, to explode in the image of the volcanoes of Chile, where Hurricane Neruda is traveling unstoppably.

As in Neruda's "Song to Bolivar," Don Pedro's elegy moves throughout Our America, as well as the other America that is the United States, but the United States of Lincoln, Thomas Payne, and that of the black population. Cuba, Panama, beautiful Mexico, Peru, that "orphan lamp" he calls Puerto Rico; and, of course, Santo Domingo, that "has a broken morning star / at the center of its navel."

Physically very fragile, in contrast to that Minotaur marvel who Whitman was, Don Pedro looks for Simón Bolívar in Neruda, his fathers, and he trusts in them for the redemption of the continent and his own:

"And you sleep, Father, as all of us men / and women of the world drink your word / from your cup of hope / and fulfill your unstoppable prophecy."

Redemption that has a price known well by Don Pedro: loneliness, which is why, as in a ritornello he repeats in "Hurricane Neruda" that Salvador Allende was left alone and also Neruda, though when a whole country takes Don Pedro's "There's a Country in the World" as a national flag, death is just an instant and the poet is reborn every time an emotional young person, boy or girl, recites trembling the verses of this poem.

In my last encounter with Don Pedro, already very ill, he declared that he was dying from the "defeat of my generation," a political defeat, but not poetic, because Don Pedro lives triumphant in the memory of his poems, accompanied, as he ought to be, by Hurricane Neruda, now I imagine a gentle breeze on the Olympus of the poets, and of course with Salvador Allende.

※

If Julia de Burgos is the national poet of Puerto Rico, only Don Pedro Mir, the son of a *borinqueña*, and the national poet of the Dominican Republic—the nation that rescued and adopted her—could measure up to writing the great Dominican poem for her.

To excite him about my proposal that he write it, I brought him all the books of Julia's poems and documents about her that I had, but convincing him wasn't easy, because Don Pedro claimed that his poetry didn't compare with Julia's. He was afraid that opposite her "Blood Hymn to Trujillo," his poem to Julia would fall short.

The first to read the initial draft was Don Juan Bosch, his longtime friend and former president of the Dominican Republic, whose enthusiastic opinion stunned Don Pedro, convincing him to keep going with the poem and finish writing it.

Who was Julia to Don Pedro? Who is she to our country?

Don Juan, Don Pedro, and Julia all were children of Puerto Rican mothers. Don Pedro and Julia shared being mulattoes—"brownies"—and of working-class origins. Don Pedro's father was a Cuban sugarcane worker; Julia's father was a peasant; and both experienced the deprivations of extreme poverty since their birth.

Don Pedro and Julia grew up near two emblematic rivers: the Rio Grande de Loíza, where Julia experienced her happiest childhood memories, and the Rio Iguamo. The difference was that Don Pedro's river was at the entrance to a port, and he could watch the ships coming and going with their load of sugarcane, while Julia's river came from the mountains, and she could only observe the water's freedom and strength, and imagine the river as her lover, as the cold embrace of early eroticism in her adolescence.

Don Juan, Julia, and Don Pedro joined the political struggles against colonialism and dictatorship at a very young age, and the three were forced into exile where their lives coincided, and their paths crossed each other's. Don Juan and Julia shared an apartment in Havana, and Don Pedro remembered hearing about her participation in the Dominican exile activities.

Unfortunately, Julia died very young and still during the Trujillo dictatorship, so not only was she unable to ever visit the Dominican Republic, but her memory was buried for decades here. Then in 1990 I managed to get an interview with Don Juan and Doctor Juan Isidro Jimenes-Grullón, the two Dominican exiles with whom she spent several years of her life in Cuba.

To commemorate the centenary of her birth in Santo Domingo was our duty, and to begin those celebrations in the country that she loved the most after Puerto Rico: Santo Domingo became our objective, and so we did. Today, the sculpture of Julia there—titled "La Nuestra" (Ours)—attracts crowds of poets and artists, young people and children, in the most beautiful little park of the colonial zone, just facing a river, the Rio Ozama, which joins the sea at the entrance of the Port of Santo Domingo.

We had also wanted a poem from the national poet of our island to the national poet of Puerto Rico, and so my second objective was to motivate Don Pedro to write it, to convince him that only he could do it, and to underscore and revive the links that tied them together, from their mothers to their ideology, from their political struggles to their visions of countryside, their hope for the future.

And so, "To Julia with No Tears" was born, because neither Julia nor Don Pedro wanted to have tears associated with their names.

CHIQUI VICIOSO
Santo Domingo, 2019

Translator's Preface:

Journey into These Poems of Pedro Mir[*]

Pedro Mir (1913–2000) is recognized as the Dominican Republic's foremost literary figure of the twentieth century. Since publishing his first poems in 1937, he sought through literature to place the Caribbean experience in global historical perspective. He also produced work in the fields of history, fiction, and art criticism and theory. In 1947, the subject of mounting suspicions of the Trujillo dictatorship, he was forced to go into exile. When he returned fifteen years later, following the death of the dictator, the poet immediately won the hearts of the Dominican people, and his poetry readings were mass public events attended by enthusiastic crowds of citizens from every walk of life. In 1982 the legislature of the Dominican Congress conferred upon him the title of National Poet, and in 1993 he received the National Prize for Literature, the highest honor a literary artist can receive in the Dominican Republic. On the occasion of Mir's death, the president of the Dominican Republic declared three days of national mourning and celebrated the poet's memory and his work: "Don Pedro will always be with us because his thinking was transcendent, and he truly fathomed the national Dominican soul."

"El huracán Neruda"—"Hurricane Neruda"—won the Annual Poetry Award given by the Secretary of Education of the Dominican Republic, in 1975, the year of the poem's original publication. This elegy was written in response to the death of Chilean poet Pablo Neruda and the military dictatorship that followed the coup in Chile and the associated death of its president, Salvador Allende, twelve days before the poet died, possibly murdered. "A Julia sin lágrimas"— "To Julia with No Tears"—was written in 1998. It is Mir's last published poem. This elegy celebrates Puerto Rican poet Julia de Burgos who gave voice to her native island and its strug-

---

[*] All translations from the Spanish are mine. —J.C.

gle for independence. A feminist in word and deed, she also spoke up for Afro-Caribbean writers. She furthered the cultural and socio-political cause of all Caribbean peoples, and for her profound contribution to this cause, she became significant to Mir.

❋

Pablo Neruda (1904–1973)—the most famous Latin American poet and a Nobel laureate—needs little introduction. The book of love poems he published at the age of twenty was a sensation, launching his poetic career. As a diplomat, he served all over the world in the consular service from 1927 on. Living in Spain during the mid-1930s, he became a close friend of Federico García Lorca and other leading Spanish poets. His engagement with the Spanish Civil War and the struggle of the Spanish people shaped him politically. His image-driven poetics, in particular that of his *Residencia en la tierra* (1935; *Residence on Earth*), had a marked influence on U.S. poetry during the 1960s and '70s, as did his blood-and-guts political poetry. Neruda and Mir both shared the idealistic vision of communism—both sided with the downtrodden in Latin America and around the world, and both championed the struggle of these people for a better life.

Mir's "Hurricane Neruda" is modeled on Neruda's tribute to Simon Bolivar, titled "Un canto para Bolívar" ("A Song for Bolivar"), which Neruda wrote for a program at the Bolivar Theatre in Mexico City, in 1941, to mark the occasion of the 111th anniversary of Bolivar's death. Here are the opening lines of the poem:

> Padre nuestro que estás en la tierra, en el agua, en el aire
> de toda nuestra extensa latitud silenciosa,
> todo lleva tu nombre, padre, en nuestra morada:
> tu apellido la caña levanta a la dulzura,
> el estaño bolívar tiene un fulgor bolívar,
> el pájaro bolívar sobre el volcán bolívar,
> la patata, el salitre, las sombras especiales,
> las corrientes, las vetas de fosfórica piedra,

todo lo nuestro viene de tu vida apagada,
tu herencia fueron ríos, llanuras, campanarios,
tu herencia es el pan nuestro de cada día, padre.

[Our Father who art in the earth, in the water, in the air
of our entire vast and silent latitude,
everything bears your name, Father, in our land:
your name the sugarcane raises to sweetness,
bolivar tin has a bolivar shine,
the bolivar bird over Bolivar Volcano,
the potato, the saltpeter, the special shadows,
the currents, the veins of phosphoric stone,
everything that is ours comes from your snuffed-out life,
your legacy was rivers, plains, bell towers,
your legacy is this our daily bread, Father.]

The poem concludes with the poet's imagined encounter with Bolivar himself, in Madrid, during the Spanish Civil War: "Father, I said to him, are you, or are you not, or who are you? / And looking toward the Mountain Barracks, he said: / 'I awake every hundred years when the people awake.'"

In his elegy here, Mir echoes Neruda's voice, not exactly verbatim but transformed, to express his particular state of mind in response to the state of affairs he calls the "neruda situation." He uses a similar echoic technique in his de Burgos poem.

❋

Julia de Burgos (1914–1953) is considered one of Puerto Rico's most important poets. Some say she is the greatest. Edward Hirsch calls her "the bedrock of Puerto Rican poetry." She grew up in the poor barrio of Santa Cruz in Carolina, and was the oldest of thirteen children; six of her youngest siblings died of malnutrition. Brilliant, aspiring, and focused, she earned a teaching certificate at the University of Puerto Rico, and worked as a teacher before moving to New York at the age of twenty-five, where she worked as a journalist, and then Cuba after a few months, where she pursued further studies at the University of Havana. Returning to New York two years later, de Burgos served as the art and culture editor for the progressive newspaper *Pueblos Hispanos* (Spanish Peoples). Her personal life was marked by several love affairs and heartbreaks. Today, she is celebrated not only as a poet, but as an advocate of Puerto Rican independence and a civil rights activist for women and Afro-Caribbean writers.

De Burgos died young and tragically in New York—she was just thirty-nine years old—collapsing on Fifth Avenue and initially taken by ambulance to a hospital that would not accept her as a patient because she was Hispanic. During her lifetime she published two collections of poems. Her third book was published the year after her death.

Mir's "To Julia with No Tears" alludes throughout it to de Burgos's most famous poems, "A Julia de Burgos" ("To Julia de Burgos") and "Río Grande de Loíza" ("Great Loíza River"). These are her signature poems. Both appeared in her first collection, *Poema en veinte surcos* (1938; Poem in Twenty Furrows). The first is a revolutionary and feminist poem in which her true inner self confronts her public self that is forced to conform to the repressive politics and social norms of her day. The second is a love poem in which the main river in the area of Puerto Rico where she grew up becomes her lover. In it she says "mi niñez fue toda un poema en el río, / y un río en el poema de mis primeros sueños" ("my childhood was all a poem in the river, / and a river in the poem of my first dreams." Both "To Julia de Burgos" and "Great Loíza River," like the other poems in her book, owe much in their poetic language to Neruda, whose *Twenty Love Poems* she knew by heart.

For the epigraph of his poem, Mir uses fragments (altered a bit) of "To Julia de Burgos," which opens this way:

> Ya las gentes murmuran que yo soy tu enemiga
> porque dicen que en verso doy al mundo tu yo.

Mienten, Julia de Burgos. Mienten, Julia de Burgos.
La que se alza en mis versos no es tu voz: es mi voz
porque tú eres ropaje y la esencia soy yo;
y el más profundo abismo se tiende entre las dos.

Tú eres fria muñeca de mentira social,
y yo, viril destello de la humana verdad.

Tú, miel de cortesana hipocresías; yo no;
que en todos mis poemas desnudo el corazón.

Tú eres como tu mundo, egoísta; yo no;
que en todo me lo juego a ser lo que soy yo.

[Now people are whispering that I am your enemy
because in poetry I give the world your me.

They lie, Julia de Burgos. They lie, Julia de Burgos.
The voice rising in my verses isn't your voice: it's mine
because you're the costume and the essence is me;
and between the two of us lies the deepest chasm.

You're just a cold doll of social falsehood,
and me, the virile flash of human truth.

You, honey of courtly hypocrisies; not me;
I bare my heart in all my poems.

You're like your world, selfish; not me;
I gamble everything to be what I am.]

Her poem continues to build as she battles with herself, and it closes with this fiery stanza:

Cuando las multitudes corran alborotadas
dejando atrás cenizas de injusticias

quemadas, y cuando con la tea de las siete virtudes,
tras los siete pecados, corran las multitudes,
contra ti, y contra todo lo injusto y lo inhumano,
yo iré en medio de ellas con la tea en la mano.

[When the multitudes run rioting in the streets
leaving behind ashes of burned injustices,
and when carrying the torch of the seven virtues,
the multitudes run after the seven sins,
against you and against everything unjust and inhuman,
I'll be right among them with the torch in my hand.]

Mir dedicated his poem to Dominican poet Chiqui Vicioso, who in the late 1970s first learned about de Burgos and felt a great solidarity with her as a Caribbean woman like herself. Beyond that, she embraced her as "a mother of humanity." In her essay "Julia de Burgos: Our Julia" (*Callaloo*, 1994), Vicioso affirms, "To pay homage to her in the Dominican Republic, the land she so loved but could never visit, and to make known her contributions to the struggle for our own true independence is not only a moral obligation but another way to proffer our love."

This obligation is precisely what Pedro Mir understood and acted on as the National Poet of the Dominican Republic. And it is this collective love that he proffers in his elegy to her.

※

With my translations here I have aimed to recreate Mir's voice in American English. Fidelity to the meaning of his Spanish guided me in rendering every line, but fidelity to the poetic quality of his verse was paramount. I wanted each translation to be an accurate equivalent as well as a beautiful poem in its own right, in order to serve him in the best possible way.

JONATHAN COHEN
New York, 2019

El huracán Neruda
elegía de una canción desesperada

A
Marino Carrera
y a Laura, su esposa,
porque apremiaban estos
versos.
      Con un clavel.

Santo Domingo, 1975

Hurricane Neruda
ELEGY WITH A SONG OF DESPAIR

To
Marino Carrera
and Laura, his wife,
because they urged these
verses.
        With a carnation.

Santo Domingo, 1975

*El estruendo bolívar sobre
el volcán Bolívar.*

Pablo Neruda, "*Canto a Bolívar*"

*The bolivar roar over
Bolivar Volcano.*

Pablo Neruda, "Song to Bolivar"

1

Han pasado las horas sobre el volcán Neruda
y el delirio y la fiebre sobre el temblor neruda
y la dormida lava de la erupción neruda
sobre el fragor de la imponente situación neruda.

Todo descansa, Padre. Sobre los marfiles
de los más viejos pianos el terciopelo duerme.

Hay una señora que se llama Luisa desde los ojos
pardos hasta el rumor de su pelo, desde su voz
de aguja hasta el final del hilo en cuyo extremo
nudo, un pequeñuelo duerme. La delicada aurora
se balancea en su mirada y se desliza en su mano,
rueda sangrando, se dirige al suelo y nos sucede
de pronto que se levanta el huracán Neruda,
la ráfaga neruda y el vórtice neruda y
                                          neruda
el vendaval,
            reconstruído por el grave
estallido de la infernal consternación neruda.

1

A lot of time has passed over Neruda Volcano
as the fevered ranting has over the neruda quake
and the sleeping lava from the neruda eruption
over the din of the imposing neruda situation.

Everything is asleep, Father. The velvet is
dead asleep on the oldest pianos' ivory keys.

There's a lady named Luisa from her brown
eyes to the sound of her hair, from her voice
like a needle to the knotted end of a thread
where a little boy sleeps. The delicate dawn
rocks in her glance and slides across her hand,
rolls bleeding, falls to the ground and all at once
we are faced with the rising Hurricane Neruda,
the neruda gust and neruda whirlwind and
                                          neruda

gale force,
            recreated by the grave
explosion of the infernal neruda dismay.

2

¿Qué ha sucedido, Padre? Súbitamente nos agravia todo.
Todo, hasta el agua misma se ha vuelto insoportable.
Los flotantes del acueducto de la cuidad, que
no hace mucho, se llevaban las nubes a las sienes y
pensaban reposadamente en tubérculos y esponjas,
de pronto se han tornado irreflexivos.
                         Se sabe ahora
de no pocos torrentes que han dormido en los bosques.
De aguas adolescentes que han trasnochado desnudas
en las calles.
              Y de turbinas de vapor que han vuelto
y devuelto el agua a sus antiguas nubes.
                               Y lo mismo
de sábanas recién lavadas que se han secado, antes
de tiempo.
             Y decididamente la misma suerte
se sabe de sudores, de naranjas y de espejos . . .

¿Qué ha sucedido, Padre? Todo ha muerto. Todo
se ha dislocado. Se ha sumergido todo. El caracol
neruda en las inmensidades de los mares neruda.
El capitán neruda en los rompientes del archipiélago
neruda.
    Y todo neruda ardiendo en la esencial madera
de aquella noche iluminada en la emoción neruda:

Quiero escribir los versos más tristes esta noche . . .

Y de pronto el celestial estruendo en la bóveda neruda.
Neruda entre los astros de la infernal dislocación neruda.

2

What's happened, Father? Suddenly everything disturbs us.
Everything, even the water itself has become unbearable.
The water lilies in the city's aqueducts, which
not long ago brought clouds to their brows and
thought calmly about tubers and sponges,
have all at once become reckless.
                                      It is now known
that several cascades have fallen asleep in the woods.
That adolescent waters have spent the night naked
in the streets.
                      And that steam turbines have turned
and returned the water to its former clouds.
                                          And as well
that freshly washed sheets are drying sooner than
expected.
              And no doubt the same fate
has been met by sweat drops, oranges and mirrors . . .

What's happened, Father? Everything is dead. Everything
is deranged. Everything flooded. The neruda
snail in the vastness of neruda seas.
Captain Neruda in the breakers of a neruda
archipelago.
              And everything neruda burning in the essential wood
of that night lit up with neruda emotion:

Tonight I want to write the saddest lines . . .

And suddenly the celestial roar in the neruda firmament.
Neruda amid the stars of the infernal neruda derangement.

3

¿Qué ha sucedido, verdadero Padre del huracán
y del volcán y la moderna lava? ¿Qué ha sucedido
en el marfil y el terciopelo de los viejos pianos
y en los rompientes de los archipiélagos?

3

What's happened, true Father of the hurricane
and the volcano and modern lava? What's happened
to the ivory and the velvet of old pianos
and to the breakers of archipelagos?

4

La historia es muy sencilla.
                          El hallazgo
neruda en las laderas de los montes
y a veces en la arena de los ríos.
Los vestigios neruda en las más altas
capas de la atmósfera y en las vértebras
de algunos individuos insaciables,
ha revelado el nexo terminante
del pueblo con las riendas de la aurora.

Feliz descubrimiento que es capaz
de emancipar regiones infinitas
de los océanos y de los desiertos
y sobre todo eliminar la noche
y los eclipses de las amapolas.

Y eso es todo. Y ha sido suficiente
para todo. Después se ha sumergido
todo. Negado y anegado todo.

Porque ha sido la aurora y no el metal
que despedaza al pueblo en sus molinos.
Sino que el pueblo mismo en situación
neruda. O si se quiere el mismo pueblo
en situación de aurora.

                Y así lo cuentan
numerosas baladas de los pueblos
y aparece en las rondas infantiles:

4

The story is very simple.
                    The neruda
evidence found on mountain sides
and at times in river sand.
Neruda traces in the highest layers
of the atmosphere and in the bones
of some insatiable individuals
have revealed the conclusive link
between the people and the reins of dawn.

A fortunate discovery capable of
emancipating infinite regions
of the oceans and deserts
and above all eliminating night
and the eclipses of poppies.

And that's all. And it has been enough
for everything. Since everything got flooded.
Everything denied and drowned.

Because it has been dawn and not metal
that is tearing the people apart in their mills.
It's just the people themselves in a neruda
situation. Or in other words the very people
in a dawn situation.

                    And so it's told
in countless ballads all around the world
and it appears in nursery rhymes:

5

La aurora tiene en su falda
varios luceros bravíos.
Uno le canta y otro le baila.
Uno en Lisboa le toca el pífano.

Le toca el triángulo.
Le toca el tímpano.

Otro le canta y uno le toca
un tamborín indochino.
Otro un timbal de Cambodia.
Y hay uno que está dormido

en los mismos párpados abiertos
de los Estados Unidos.
No es Cuba, naturalmente.
Ni un Panamá ni un México herido

con todo lo que en sus respectivas
aguas hay de canal y de río.
Ni este Perú rescatándose.
Ni esta Argentina en peligro.

Y
menos
Santo Domingo
que tiene roto un lucero
en el centro del ombligo.

Ni siquiera esa lámpara huérfana
de luz que se llama Puerto Rico,
que ya se sabe que alumbra nuevos
huevos de sombra en su viejo nido.

5

Dawn has a free-spirited band
of morning stars on her lap.
One sings to her and another dances.
One in Lisbon plays the fife.

One plays the triangle.
One plays the drum.

Another sings to her and one plays
an Indochinese tambourine.
Another a Cambodian barrel drum.
And there is one that fell asleep

right on the open eyelids
of the United States.
It isn't Cuba, naturally.
Nor Panama or wounded Mexico

with everything in their respective
waters forming canal and river.
Nor Peru saving itself.
Nor Argentina in danger.

And
least of all
Santo Domingo
that has a broken morning star
at the center of its navel.

Not even that orphan lamp
of light called Puerto Rico,
known already to shine on fresh
eggs of darkness in its old nest.

Ni siquiera son los negros
de los Estados Unidos.
Sino la nación entera
de Thomas Payne y de Lincoln,

desde las costas atlánticas
hasta el búfalo extinguido,
desde el resuello del jazz
hasta el pullman del Pacífico,

la que tiene entre sus párpados
abiertos los luceros dormidos.
Y uno le canta y otro le baila.
Y otro le brilla en el pueblo mismo.

Y otro le salta y otro le toca
la sinfonía medio dormido,
le toca el triángulo,
le rompe el tímpano,

en los mismos párpados abiertos
de los Estados Unidos.

It isn't even the blacks
of the United States.
Nor the whole nation
of Thomas Paine and Lincoln,

from the Atlantic coast
to the extinct buffalo,
from the breath of jazz
to the Pacific Pullman car,

the nation with sleeping stars
between its open eyelids.
And one sings to her and another dances.
And another shines on the people themselves.

And another leaps and another plays
the symphony half asleep,
one plays the triangle,
one pounds the drum,

right on the open eyelids
of the United States.

6

Y esto nos explica la situación neruda.
Dicen que Salvador Allende era de color de rosa
con algunas tonalidades aborígenes y suaves
matices amarillos sobre ondulaciones negras . . .

Y cuentan que tenía ascendencia británica
de obreros y también de campesinos celtas
y labriegos eslavos en las que fueron sus venas.

Y que corrían en su sangre antecesores monegascos
y raíces indostánicas mezcladas con italianas,
en el lívido intervalo que media en primavera,
entre una cepa escandinava y los mineros
araucanos más trabajados en el cobre.

                                              Y además
todo envuelto en un contorno delicado de velamen
español, muy nuevo mundo y lusitano, en un pleno
y desencadenadamente lúcido contenido chileno
totalmente encapotado por la bandera de Chile.

Eso dicen . . .

Y quieren decir que era un orgullo de la humanidad
entera y que tenía toda su sangre comprometida
y que en ella se hallaba comprometida la humanidad
entera.

Y entonces hubo que arrancar a Salvador Allende
de las entrañas de la humanidad entera.

        La aurora tenía en su falda
        varios luceros en Chile
        y unos bailaban en el cobre
        y otros cantaban en el salitre

6

And this explains the neruda situation.
They say that Salvador Allende looked rosy
with some Amerindian coloring and light
yellow tones on black waves . . .

And they claim he had British working-class
ancestry as well as the blood of Celtic peasants
and Slavic farmhands in what were his veins.

And that Monacan ancestors ran in his blood
and he had Hindustani roots mixed with Italian,
in the pale interval that happens at springtime,
between Scandinavian stock and Araucanian
overworked copper miners.

                                        And besides
everything wrapped in a delicate case of Spanish
sail cloth, very New World and Lusitanian, with full
and unrestrainedly clear Chilean content
totally shrouded in the flag of Chile.

That's what they say . . .

And what they mean is that he was a pride of all
humanity and had committed his blood totally
and that in his blood all humanity was
committed.

And then Salvador Allende had to be extracted
from the guts of all humanity.

        Dawn once had on her lap
        several morning stars in Chile
        and some danced on copper
        and others sang on saltpeter

Y entonces hubo que desprender a Salvador Allende
de las entrañas de la humanidad
                              entera.
Y eso es todo.

Y cuentan que en ciertas noches de perfecta oscuridad
se escucha una canción desesperada:

And then Salvador Allende had to be removed
from the guts of all
                    humanity.
And that's it.

And they claim that on certain perfectly dark nights
you can hear a song of despair:

7

¡En Chile! ¡No hay un minuto que perder
en Chile! Que hay una rosa en el vergel
peruano con toda una arrogancia de canal
panameño que nunca debe florecer

¡en Chile! ¡No hay un instante que perder
en Chile! Antes de que empiecen las misas
de Camilo Torres y los poemas del Cardenal
Ernesto o Ernesto Cardenal

¡en Chile! Hay que incendiar a Chile!
Antes de que en Chile el presidente rojo
o el presidente amarillo o el presidente
negro decidan amanecer ¡en Chile!

  (Arminda, ábreme la puerta
  que todo es nuevo
  que ahora nace una espiga
  llamada el pueblo)

¡en Chile! Que esos muchachos que ponían
claveles en los fusiles del Pentágono
en la precisa ciudad de Washington
como nos cuenta TIME no deberán crecer

  (Ay doña Arminda madame
  Arminda señora Arminda
  con los luceros que hay en tus ojos
  podría la aurora acarrear disturbios)

¡en Chile! Ni en una calle ni en una esquina
ni en las escuelas que hay en los parques

7

In Chile! There isn't a minute to lose
in Chile! There's a rose in the Peruvian
garden as all-out arrogant as the Panama
Canal that should never flower

In Chile! There isn't a moment to lose
in Chile! Before the masses of Camilo Torres
begin and the poems of Cardinal Ernesto
that is, Ernesto Cardenal, begin

In Chile! It's time to burn Chile!
Before the red president in Chile
or the yellow president or the black
chooses to start the day, in Chile!

> (Arminda, open the door for me
> because everything is new
> because a tassel is sprouting
> called the people)

In Chile! Because those kids who stuck
carnations in the Pentagon's rifles
right there in Washington, D.C.,
according to TIME won't grow up

> (Ay Doña Arminda Madam
> Arminda Señora Arminda
> with those stars in your eyes
> the dawn could spark riots)

In Chile! Not on a street or on a corner
or in the schools that are in the parks

(Ay, Arminda, ábreme la puerta
que no es que le tema al cuartel
ni que le tema a los pueblos
que luchan junto con él
sino que Arminda ábreme la puerta
que estoy sufriendo

Que una verde cotorra se fue para Portugal:
Dame la patita, la cotorrita viene de Portugal

Arminda, ábreme la puerta
que en su pico trae un clavel
y un incendio colonial)

¡En Chile, en Chile, en Chile no hay un solo
        minuto
     que perder.

>   (Ay, Arminda, open the door
>   it's not that I'm afraid of the garrison
>   or that I'm afraid of all the people
>   who are fighting alongside him
>   come on, Arminda, open the door
>   because I'm hurting bad

So a little green parrot flies off to Portugal:
Give me your little foot, little parrot from Portugal

>   Arminda, open the door for me
>   because in its beak it has a carnation
>   and a colonial blaze)

In Chile, in Chile, in Chile there isn't a single
                minute
                      to lose!

8

Y así avanzaron en Chile con esta canción desesperada.

                      Y así derramaron
toda la sangre de Salvador Allende por las calles
de Santiago de Chile.

                Derramaron sangre chilena
en su más pura cepa andaluza y berebere con latidos
keniatas y pulsaciones bretonas de glóbulos egipcios
e iraquíes.
            Corrieron por la acera y se mezclaron
en el polvo con la palpitaciones de sangre japonesa,
turquestana y hebrea, húngara y moscovita.

                        Formaban
pequeños pozos donde palpitaba toda la América
incluyendo fragantes borbotones de Oregón, del "black
belt" y de Nebraska con diluídos pulsos canadienses.

De aztecas y de mayas, de culíes hindúes, de zíngaros
y gitanos montenegrinos y coronarias martiniqueñas.

Y claveles purpúreos de Nigeria y rosas de Francia
y de Cayena se unieron en todas las esquinas y formaron
una sola corriente de sangre de toda la humanidad,
vertida del torrente chileno de Salvador Allende . . .

Y aunque la sangre derramada era amarilla y naturalmente
blanca y desde luego cobriza e inevitablemente negra,
la ciudad se hizo más roja que nunca.
                      Más carmesí
que nunca. Más colorada y bermellón que nunca.

8

And so they advanced in Chile with this song of despair.

                              And so they spilled
all the blood of Salvador Allende in the streets
of Santiago de Chile.

                       They spilled Chilean blood
of its purest Andalusian and Berber strain with Kenyan
beats and Breton pulsations from Egyptian and Iraqi
corpuscles.
         Palpitating Japanese blood, Turkestani and
Jewish, Hungarian and Muscovite ran along the sidewalk
with them and they mixed together in the dust.

                                    They formed
small pools where all of America throbbed
including fragrant spurts from Oregon, the *black
belt* and Nebraska with faint Canadian pulses.

From Aztecs and Mayans, Hindu coolies, Romani
and Montenegrin gypsies and Martinican coronaries.

And purple carnations from Nigeria and roses from France
and Guiana gathered at all the streetcorners and formed
a single stream of blood flowing from all humanity,
shed from the Chilean torrent of Salvador Allende . . .

And though the blood spilled was yellow and naturally
white and very much copper colored and inevitably black,
the city became redder than ever.
                         More crimson
than ever. More scarlet and vermilion than ever.

Y nunca la rosa fue tan roja como en Santiago entonces.
Ninguna boca de trapecista inglesa fue más enrojecida para
   el espectáculo.
Ninguna espada de torero andaluz ni lámpara de guardavía.

Más purpúreo que nunca, como Santiago en esos días,
lo fue, jamás, el clavel en su etapa sangrienta.

La sangre universal de Salvador Allende inundó a todo Chile
y siguió creciendo en el recuerdo humano y en la estirpe
vegetal y en el instinto de todos los seres inanimados.

Y no habrá ningún nivel que soporte esa creciente.
    Ni corazón que le impida latir a ese recuerdo.
    Ni que se aparte de él.

And a rose was never as red as it was in Santiago then.
No mouth of a female English trapeze artist was redder for the
    circus.
No sword of an Andalusian bullfighter or signalman's lamp.

The carnation in its bloody stage was more purple
than ever before, like Santiago in those days.

The universal blood of Salvador Allende flooded all of Chile
and kept growing in human memory and in the plant
life and in the instinct of all inanimate beings.

And there will never be a level that can hold that growth.
        Or a heart that can stop that memory from beating.
        Or turn away from him.

9

Y cuando ardiendo la fruta se prodiga
copiosamente en el tonel y brota
la muchacha sonriente y en la espiga

de los cañaverales, gota a gota
se destila el sudor, de la garganta
del pueblo sale su más limpia nota

que llega a América Latina y canta.
Y de repente el huracán Neruda
del vórtice neruda se levanta.

Y en el sudeste asiático la aguda
contradicción despedaza la historia
y en la noche neruda el sol neruda:

triunfo en la vida y en la muerte gloria.
Y en Europa una siembra de fusiles
con un clavel neruda en la victoria.

Mi corazón y el corazón de miles
de corazones creen en tu poesía,
Padre nuestro que estás mirando Chiles

presentes y futuros. La poesía,
tu poesía, anunció que el capitán
Bolívar capitán del pueblo, volvería

cada cien años con el huracán
Neruda envuelto en la cabeza y cien
años de Chile y de tu muerte van.

9

And when the copious fermenting fruit
fills the wooden vat and the smiling girl
emerges from it—and in the tassels

of sugarcane fields, drop by drop
sweat is distilled—from the people's
throat comes their clearest note

that reaches Latin America and sings.
And all of a sudden Hurricane Neruda
arises from the neruda whirlwind.

And in Southeast Asia the sharp
contradiction shatters history
and in neruda night neruda sun:

triumph in life and glory in death.
And in Europe a sowing of guns
with a neruda carnation on victory day.

My heart and the heart of thousands
of hearts believe in your poetry,
our Father who keeps an eye on Chiles

now and in the future. Poetry,
your poetry, announced that Captain
Bolívar, the people's captain, would return

every hundred years with Hurricane
Neruda whirling around his head, and here are
a hundred years of Chile and your death.

Otros dos siglos pasarán también.
Si no es porque esta noche el mundo entero
torna y retorna de tu muerte, amén.

Del más remoto punto del acero,
de la cuenca del cobre y de la nata
del hierro en el crisol y del primero

de los metales y después la plata,
pasando el manganeso y la bauxita,
un cinturón de manos se dilata

y en tu exacta violencia se da cita,
y traspasa en los términos humanos
la diplomacia de la dinamita.

Y en todos los caminos brotan manos
tuyas y abiertas a un mundo mejor.
Y entre la espiga y los futuros granos

y las manos que sudan y el sudor,
hay un Chile que torna al cataclismo
y un Chile que retorna al resplandor.

Un Chile más neruda en el abismo,
más chileno en la fiebre y más neruda
y universal que el universo mismo,

bajo la gris consternación neruda.
Y de repente el sólido huracán
Neruda, emprende el vértigo neruda
y regresa cantando el Capitán.

Another two centuries will pass as well.
If not it's because tonight the whole world
keeps coming back to your death, amen.

From the farthest tip of the blade,
from the copper mines and molten
iron in the crucible and the first

of the metals and then silver,
passing the manganese and bauxite,
a belt of hands grows long

and gathers in your exact violence,
and conveys in human terms
the diplomacy of dynamite.

And on all the roads your hands
emerge and open to a better world.
And amid the tassels and future grains

and sweating hands and sweat,
there's a Chile that turns to cataclysm
and a Chile that returns to splendor.

A more neruda Chile in the abyss,
more Chilean in fervor and more neruda
and universal than the universe itself,

under the grey neruda consternation.
And all of a sudden firm Hurricane
Neruda sets off a neruda blast of air
and the Captain is back, singing.

10

Entonces podemos anunciar que hemos entrado estrepitosamente
en ese gran sistema de estupor y sacrificio que denominamos
una aurora

> para todos los hombres,
> para todos los países,
> para todos los tiempos

y desde luego para todo sistema planetario y universo cósmico.

> Para todas las palomas,
> para todos los gavilanes
> y para todas sus aventuras
> y temperaturas genitales.

I

Precisamente en esas páginas inaugurales de los grandes libros
donde las generaciones inscriben sus violencias natales. Y
donde las civilizaciones inventan sus sistemas de cálculo:

> cincuenta y algas
> sesenta y látigos
> setenta y vísceras
> ochenta y síncopas

Y en lugar de noventa y uno:

noventa y razas, noventa y rosas, noventa y risas y fracciones
de muerte fina, divisiones de escape y ecuaciones de júbilo,
elevadas a la indómita potencia que multiplica el tronco
de los pueblos, pasadas las tormentas y las conflagraciones.

10

Then we can proclaim that we have spectacularly entered
into that great system of amazement and sacrifice we call
a dawn

>> for all men,
>> for all countries,
>> for all times

and of course for the whole planetary system and cosmic universe.

>> For all doves,
>> for all hawks
>> and for all their affairs
>> and genital temperatures.

I

Precisely in those opening pages of great books
where generations record their violent regimes. And
where civilizations invent their counting systems:

>> fifty-algae
>> sixty-whips
>> seventy-guts
>> eighty-faints

> And instead of ninety-one:

ninety-races, ninety-roses, ninety-laughs plus fractions
of fine death, divisions of escape and equations of joy,
raised to the irrepressible power that multiplies the stock
of peoples, once the storms and conflagrations are over.

II

Porque la aurora no es necesariamente un círculo absoluto.
Reflexionando sobre acontecimientos y pasadas noches
se ve cómo una esfera de circunstancias y de mariposas
colocada en el tiempo se convierte en indómita conducta.

De manera que lo que impone el tránsito brusco de un sistema
hacia una calidad inesperada y venturosa, no siempre indica
la dirección de las bibliotecas o el canal de los circuítos
    electrónicos.
                    Porque sucede que no siempre se sube a la colina
subiendo la colina.
                           Los pequeños sonrojos del crepúsculo,
las manos que prefieren agua fresca, el arroyuelo mismo
y el ansia de retorno, son un componente de la altura.

La marcha de la aurora es torno y retorno en las colinas.

Y el mismo caracol es un ejemplo: torna y retorna en espiral
y de improviso desemboca en la vida. Y el ejemplo más puro
                      es la propia vida.

Y ella impone reemplazar la esfera del reloj con la imperante
esfera de la aurora.
                  Imprimir al redondo vals de sus agujas
el despavorido galope del tiempo
                              con su polvareda de cambios
que se suceden sorpresivamente mordiéndole las horas
ondulantes, ni un minuto antes ni un minuto después,
en Europa, en Australasia, en Oceanía,
como si se tratara de un tropel de caballos,
en América, en sus praderas desbocadas,
                                  mordidos
en la cola con violencia de cambio por un chispazo
flagelante de la aurora.

II

Because dawn is not necessarily an absolute circle.
Reflecting on events and past nights
we can see how a sphere of circumstances and butterflies
positioned in time becomes irrepressible behavior.

So that what demands the abrupt transition of a system
toward a surprising fortunate quality doesn't always explain
the address of libraries or the pathway of electronic
   circuits.
             Because it happens we don't always get up the hill
going up the hill.
             The slight blushes of twilight,
the hands that prefer fresh water, the stream itself
and longing for return, are a part of the peak.

The dawn's movement is a circling back in the hills.

And the very snail is an example: it circles back in a spiral
and by surprise ends up at life. And the purest example
                    is life itself.

And it demands replacing the clock's dial with the ruling
dial of the dawn.
            Stamping on the round waltz of its hands
the terrified gallop of time
                    with its dust cloud of changes
that suddenly follow one another biting the rolling
hours, not a minute before or a minute after,
in Europe, in Australia, in Oceania,
as if it were a stampeding herd of horses,
in America, on its wide-open prairies,
                    bites
to the butt with the violence of change by a whipping
spark of dawn.

       Y por la serpiente o corriente
del petróleo y de la gasolina.
      Y por una muchedumbre de pavorosas fieras
metálicas, el cromo, el aluminio, el molibdeno,
y el tungsteno y el acero y el iridio.
            Y por un inexacto
infinito de billetes de banco en estado de ventolina
en los desfiladeros del mercado.
             Y por la explosión
de la natalidad que multiplica los fantasmas. Y
por millones de automóviles pasando por el ojo del camello,
y autobuses atestados de colegiales y colegialas
y de obreros y también de locomotoras atestadas
de militares, de sacerdotes y de camareros uniformados,
que tornan y retornan formando en espiral la catástrofe
que tarde o temprano desemboca en la vida.

III

Y cuando toda esta turbamulta alucinante crece
en todas las raíces y las ramas del mundo, inopinadamente
crece también el pavor y crece la desesperación y crispan
el odio y la furia sus garras y caen sobre el Palacio
de la Moneda de Chile, y los cañones disparan al revés,
en dirección de la aurora, con la noche a la espalda
y estalla de repente la infernal consternación neruda y
  la desarticulación
neruda, en todos los ejes dislocados del mecanismo celeste.

Y cuando el poeta desciende de una manera o de la otra. Y es
enterrado y desenterrado y enterrado de nuevo no se sabe
dónde, y arropado en las sombras de la infamia no se sabe
cuándo, no se sabe cómo,
         y sobre su recinto solitario
se sobrepone un tacón de hierro
           y sobre el recinto
solitario de Salvador Allende, su lector favorito,

                And by the snake or flow
of oil and gasoline.
              And by an abundance of terrifying metal
wild beasts, chromium, aluminum, molybdenum,
and tungsten and steel and iridium.
                                  And by an approximate
infinity of banknotes blown by a sudden gust of wind
in the market's narrow aisles.
                          And by the explosion
of the birth rate that multiplies ghosts. And
by millions of cars passing through the eye of the camel,
and buses packed with schoolboys and schoolgirls
and workers and also of locomotive trains packed
with soldiers, with priests and with uniformed waiters,
all keep coming back in a spiral forming the catastrophe
that sooner or later leads to life.

                          III

And when all this amazing multitude believes
in all the roots and branches of the world, unexpectedly
believes the terror as well and believes the despair and
when hatred and fury clench their fists and the people seize
La Moneda Palace in Chile, and cannons fire in reverse,
in the direction of dawn, with night at its back, and the
infernal neruda dismay suddenly blows up and the neruda
    crippling disarray,
in all the deranged axes of the celestial mechanism.

And when the poet descends in some manner or another. And he
is buried and exhumed and buried again no one knows
where, and wrapped in the shadows of infamy no one knows
when, no one knows how,
                          and on his solitary plot
grinds an iron heel
                    and on the solitary
plot of Salvador Allende, his favorite reader,

se sobrepone un tacón de hierro que recibe en su pecho
      la humanidad entera,

y cuando se descubre que la vida torna y retorna en espiral
y que todos estos descensos son un componente de la altura

y cuando el caracol neruda es un ejemplo en las inmensidades
de los mares neruda. Y Salvador Allende es un ejemplo
en los rompientes de los archipiélagos neruda. Y cuando el ejemplo
      más puro es la propia vida...

entonces podemos anunciar que hemos entrado estrepitosamente
en ese gran sistema de escalofrío que denominamos una infancia

      una inminencia

      una consagración

en las aguas ardientes y tormentosas de una indómita aurora

      Para todos los hombres,
      para todos los países,
      para todas las épocas

y desde luego implicando en ello a todo el sistema planetario
y a todas las instituciones desconocidas del universo cósmico.

grinds an iron heel that all humanity takes
>   on its chest,

and when it's revealed that life circles back in a spiral
and that all these descents are a part of the peak

and when the neruda snail is an example of the vastness
of neruda seas. And Salvador Allende is an example
in the breakers of neruda archipelagos. And when the
>   purest example is life itself . . .

then we can proclaim that we have spectacularly entered
into that great system of trembling we call an infancy

>   a becoming

>   a founding

in the fiery storm-tossed waters of an irrepressible dawn

>   For all men,
>   for all countries,
>   for all ages

and of course as implied here for the whole planetary system
and for every unknown institution of the cosmic universe.

11

Y eso es todo. Han pasado las horas y han caído
abatidas por la espalda a los pies del calendario.
Las naranjas reanudan su bohemia amarilla, después
de una estación acidulada en los confines
de una implacable disciplina verde. Las sábanas
recién lavadas, que han dado a luz antes de tiempo,
retornan a la brisa todavía manchadas
         de estupor.

Y lo mismo sucede a las banderas y a las lavanderas.

Y eso es todo. En Managua, en Wisconsin, en Ilo-Ilo
ulula el viento, cargado de frecuencias telegráficas
e instintos masculinos. En Santo Domingo de Guzmán
las palmeras cogidas de la mano recorren las nuevas
avenidas, que se sumergen debajo de otras avenidas
para alcanzar los puentes, mientras los suburbios
urbanizan sus bucles, cambian el estilo de los surtidores,
y tú dices
  "merde" porque mi corazón no puede más
  porque nuestros corazones no pueden más
  en un mundo que deja morir solos sus heroes.

Y tus versos golpean la pared de la aurora. Y el eco
parece morir cien veces detrás de esa pared y detrás
de las metrópolis y detrás de las naciones subdesarrolladas
y detrás de las zonas turísticas.
     Cierto.
        Cierto.

Y los héroes, con los ojos abiertos, siguen muriendo solos en Chile.
En Chile y otras partes. Cierto.
Pero todo ha cambiado, Padre.

11

And that's all. Much time has gone by and fallen
hard from the head to the foot of the calendar.
Oranges are back to their bohemian yellow, after
a season turned sour in the confines
of a relentless green discipline. The freshly
washed sheets, which gave birth prematurely,
are back in the breeze but still stained
                                              with amazement.

The same thing is true for flags and washerwomen.

And that's all. In Managua, in Wisconsin, in Ilo-Ilo
the wind howls, heavy with telegraph frequencies
and male instincts. In Santo Domingo de Guzmán
palm trees holding hands are strolling along new
avenues, which dip below other avenues
to reach the bridges, while the suburbs
urbanize their loops, change the style of fountains,
and you say
> *"merde" because my heart can't take any more*
> *because our hearts just can't take any more*
> *in a world that lets its heroes die alone.*

And your lines hit the wall of dawn. And the echo
seems to die a hundred times behind that wall and behind
the capital cities and behind the underdeveloped nations
and behind the tourist zones.
                      It's true.
                            It's true.

And heroes, with their eyes open, are still dying alone in Chile.
In Chile and elsewhere. It's true.
But everything has changed, Father.

        La muerte misma ha cambiado
de soledad.
      La vida misma se nutre de la misma muerte.
Y en los grandes silencios y en las grandes soledades
nacen denodadamente nuevos héroes de los muertos solos,
multitudes de nuevos héroes más robustos y menos solos,
en Chile y otras partes. Cierto.

    Y sus corazones ahora pueden más
   y nuestros corazones ahora pueden más
en un mundo completamente iluminado por sus héroes.

Y no valdrán, para decirlo parodiando a Rioja,
   las puntas de las armas y la púrpura hermosa
   a detener un punto la ejecución del alba presurosa.

Vendrán otros poetas y una joven poesía
jamás escrita o escuchada, completamente
insólita, íntegramente desencadenada
en maderas sonoras y piedras desconocidas,
en cristales inéditos y transparencias
únicas, de celulosa y derivados del petróleo,
construída por la nueva juventud y la nueva
ancianidad que mira hacia el futuro.

Desde tí, de tu madera de nave descubridora.
Vendrán otros poemas de amor y de alegría
de un ruego inesperado y esperanza absoluta
que tejerán las manos y serán muchas manos
que la alzarán al pueblo y serán muchos pueblos.
Y el idioma del mundo serán esos poemas
que las doncellas bravas llevarán al mercado
para comprar con ellos metales inauditos
y goces increíbles y pájaros de fuego.

                              Death itself has changed
solitude.
            Life itself is nourished by this very death.
And in the great silences and in the great solitudes
new heroes are bravely born from the dead alone,
multitudes of new heroes more tough and less alone,
in Chile and elsewhere. It's true.

            And their hearts now can take more
         and our hearts now can take more
in a world completely illuminated by its heroes.

And to say it parodying Rioja, the tips of weapons
        and the beautiful purple won't allow the prompt
        dawn execution to stop in the nick of time.

Other poets and a youthful poetry will come,
never before written or heard, completely
unusual, totally unrestrained
in sonorous wood and unknown stones,
in unpublished crystals and unique
clearness, from cellulose and oil byproducts,
constructed by the new youth and the new
old age that looks toward the future.

Since you, from your discovery ship's wood.
Other poems of love and happiness will come
from an unforeseen plea and absolute hope
that hands will weave and there will be many hands,
stirring hope in the people and there will be many peoples.
And these poems will be the language of the world
that brave maidens will take to the marketplace
to buy with them unheard-of metals
and treats unreal and firebirds.

12

Y tú descansa, Padre, que todos los hombres
y las mujeres del mundo bebemos tu palabra
en tu copa de esperanza
y alzamos tu indomable profecía.

12

And you sleep, Father, as all of us men
and women of the world drink your word
from your cup of hope
and fulfill your unstoppable prophecy.

Y,

13

                para dejar constancia
y para que no quede la más mínima duda, consagramos
y firmamos y sellamos esta época muda por los años
                  de gracia y de desgracia
                  de mil novecientos neruda.

And,

13

          for the record
and so that not the slightest doubt remains, we recognize
and we sign and seal this age that's been mute for years
              of grace and disgrace
                  in nineteen hundred neruda.

A Julia sin lágrimas

Y
a Sherezada Vicioso
(Chiqui)
progenitora de este poema,
y de la lluvia, las frutas y la
gracia de este país.

Santo Domingo, 1998

To Julia with No Tears

*And
to Sherezada Vicioso
(Chiqui)
progenitor of this poem,
and of the rain, fruits and
charm of this country.*

Santo Domingo, 1998

Mienten, Julia de Burgos. Mienten, Julia de Burgos.
La que se alza en mis versos no es tu voz: es mi voz . . .
(. . .)
contra ti y contra todo lo injusto y lo inhumano
yo iré en medio de ellas con mi tea en la mano . . .

Julia de Burgos, "A Julia de Burgos"

They lie, Julia de Burgos. They lie, Julia de Burgos.
The voice rising in my verses isn't your voice: it's mine . . .
(. . .)
against you and against everything unjust and inhuman
I'll be right there among them with my torch in hand . . .

Julia de Burgos, "To Julia de Burgos"

1

Por un camino de sal que tiene el sol
se llega al Mar Caribe
por un camino de sol que tiene el mar
entonces Puerto Rico

y pronto
porque el aire es transparente
y el agua clara

y además está muy próximo
Santo Domingo

ciertamente se hace necesario
conocerse a sí mismo y jugárselo todo

(la moneda en el aire y el instante del vuelo
en el tapete rojo que cubre los tejados
y hasta el bastón callejero de los faroles
nocturnos en los costados de las aceras
de la ciudad) si es necesario
para no disputarse consigo mismo
porque ya está muy cerca
el Cementerio de Carolina en Puerto Rico
y allí reposan juntas Julia de Burgos
y Julia de Burgos a quien también llamaban
Julia de Burgos
porque en las mil y una noches todo es mentira
y Julia de Burgos nunca será Julia de Burgos
porque si hay una cosa jamás controvertida
es que Julia de Burgos era inexorablemente
Julia de Burgos
cuando miró hacia el mundo y se tiró a la calle
con un río en la mano
(que era su látigo)

1

By a road of salt that belongs to the sun
the Caribbean Sea is reached
by a road of sun that belongs to the sea
then Puerto Rico

and fast
because the air is transparent
and the water clear

and what's more Santo Domingo
is right nearby

of course it becomes necessary
to know yourself and gamble everything

(the coin in the air and the time of its flight
over the red carpet covering the rooftops
and even the walking stick of the nocturnal
streetlights along the curbs of the sidewalks
of the city) if it is necessary
for not arguing with yourself
because the Carolina Cemetery
in Puerto Rico is very close
and there Julia de Burgos rests together
with Julia de Burgos who they also called
Julia de Burgos
because in the one thousand and one nights everything is a lie
and Julia de Burgos will never be Julia de Burgos
because if there's one thing that can't be denied
it's that Julia de Burgos was unstoppably
Julia de Burgos
when she looked at the world and took to the street
with a river in her hand
(that was her whip)

y una tea en la mano
(que era su pueblo)
porque era entonces la verdadera
Julia de Burgos

porque era entonces
por lo emancipado y por lo independiente
y no por lo triste y lo desgarrado
ni por lo disipado desgarradoramente
Julia de Burgos

and a torch in her hand
(that was her people)
because then she was the real
Julia de Burgos

because then she was
for emancipation and for independence
and not for sadness and tatters
nor for dissipation being tattered
Julia de Burgos

2

Y tal fue la voz que alimentaba el eco y tal
el ruido de la semilla hasta hacerse arrozal

la multitud de voces que la garganta puebla
y el sudor de los ríos para volverse niebla

y las manos sonoras y las bocas y tal
el desparpajo de la competencia nupcial

del Río Grande de Loíza que en su secreta
alcoba la niña borincana se hizo poeta

y en su secreta alcoba se hizo borincana
no por nacer ni por establecerse antillana

ni porque en sus corrientes inscribió su apellido
y se lanzó a cantar y se olvidó del olvido

sino porque en los coros de la aurora trigueña
su voz hizo a Puerto Rico más puertorriqueña

y a Santo Domingo más voluntarioso y tal
fue la bulliciosa espiga de su verso inmortal

que al fin nos hizo a todos más puertorriqueños
a condición de hacernos más voluntad que ensueños
y a convertir en roca las iras de cristal

2

And hers was the voice that fed the echo and so
the popping of seed destined to be a rice field

the multitude of voices that populate her throat
and the sweat of rivers turning soon into mist

and the resounding hands and the mouths and so
her very daring poise at the bridal competition

of the Rio Grande de Loíza in whose secret
bedroom the Borinquen girl became a poet

and in its secret bedroom she became Borinquen
not by birth nor just by growing up Antillean

nor because she wrote her name in its currents
and started to sing and forgot about oblivion

but because in the choirs of cinnamon-skin dawn
her voice made Puerto Rico more Puerto Rican

and made Santo Domingo more strong willed and so
it was the noisy bell-tongue of her immortal verse

that ultimately made us all more Puerto Rican
on the condition we become more will than daydreams
and turn our crystal angers into rock

3

Por un camino que tiene el sol
y también por otros muchos caminos
se llega al Mar Caribe

                por el aire
como llegaron las primeras semillas
              por el agua
como llegaron las primeras zozobras
              por el fuego
que a veces despoblaba y a veces
rompía las cadenas y las calles rompía
y se tragaba las ciudades y se tragaba
              las biblias
y también por correspondencia marítima
y también estremecidos por los memoriales
          y sobre todo por la mentira

éstas han sido tierras que pertenecen
al mar y por supuesto
no es cuestión de flotar
como las goletas en las ondas salinas

(no es cuestión de que Julia de Burgos
se nos vuelva amorosa con Julia de Burgos)

Por los caminos de sol que traga el mar
y por todos los caminos
se llega al Mar Caribe

y es cuestión de la sangre y el sudor
y de morirse de hambre
y por lo mismo de quebrar las piedras
reventando una piedra contra otra piedra
y reventando a Julia de Burgos contra Julia

3

By a road that belongs to the sun
and also by many other ways
the Caribbean Sea is reached

            by air
as the first seeds arrived
            by water
as the first capsized boats arrived
            by fire
that at times depopulated and at times
broke apart chains and broke apart streets
and swallowed cities and swallowed
            bibles
and also by maritime correspondence
and also trembling by the memorials
      and above all by the lie

these have been lands that belong
to the sea and of course
there's no question of floating
like schooners on the salty waves

(there's no question that Julia de Burgos
returns to us with affection for Julia de Burgos)

By roads of sun the sea swallows
and by all the ways
the Caribbean Sea is reached

and there's a question of blood and sweat
and of dying of hunger
and for the same reason of shattering stones
smashing one stone against another stone
and smashing Julia de Burgos against Julia

de Burgos a quien también llamaban Julia
de Puerto Rico y ahora llaman también
del Mar Caribe

aunque a veces una voz más presuntuosa
quiebra unos vidrios en su garganta
para llamarla Julia de Santo Domingo

de Burgos who they also called Julia
of Puerto Rico and now also Julia
of the Caribbean Sea

although at times a more presumptuous voice
shatters glasses to pieces in its throat
for calling her Julia de Santo Domingo

4

    Porque
la Cuestión de Santo Domingo
como la llaman en cancillerías
es la misma cuestión de Puerto Rico
y ha sido siempre la misma cuestión
del Mar Caribe
y si se sigue caminando ocurre
que aparece en todos los arrecifes
y debajo de las minas y las plantaciones
y encima de las azoteas y los edificios
y naturalmente en el corazón de las nubes
que es otro de los caminos de las espadas
que penden sobre el destino del Mar Caribe

porque esta cuestión tiene ya numerosas
mariposas y carreteras

a Puerto Rico primeramente
me la hicieron esclava
después cafetalera
después azucarera
después petroquímica y medio petrolera
y por fin le llenaron la boca
de amores desgraciados
y la dejaron morir en Nueva York
en 106 y Quinta Avenida exactamente
y miserablemente
como una hispana cualquiera
y a todos se nos murió un pedazo
devorados por esa terrible enfermedad
llamada la Cuestión de Santo Domingo
así descrita en los archivos diplomáticos
porque es muy fácil ser atacados

4

        Because
the Question of Santo Domingo
as they call it in ministries
is the same question of Puerto Rico
and has always been the same question
of the Caribbean Sea
and if you keep walking it happens
to appear on all the reefs
and under the mines and plantations
and on top of roofs and buildings
and naturally in the heart of the clouds
that is another of the ways of swords
that hang over the fate of the Caribbean Sea

because this question already has numerous
butterflies and highways

first off as for Puerto Rico
they made her a slave
then a coffee planter
then a sugar refinery
then a petrochemical factory and half an oil company
and finally they filled her mouth
with unhappy loves
and they let her die in New York
precisely at 106th Street and Fifth Avenue
and miserably
like any Hispanic girl
and a piece of us all died with her
devoured by that terrible disease
called the Question of Santo Domingo
as described in the diplomatic archives
because it is very easy to be victims

y después morir a causa del amor
como una muy común América Latina

pero de todos modos Julia de Burgos no
definitivamente no
verdaderamente porque no

and then to die of love
like a very common Latin America

but nonetheless Julia de Burgos no
definitely no
absolutely because no

5

Pero
¿por qué me la hicieron salir
desnuda del Río Grande de Loíza
y la echaron a andar tras el amor
por las esquinas de La Habana?
¿La Habana? La Habana era entonces
un maremoto capitalista lleno de espectadores
y todos naufragábamos frente al Malecón
La Habana era una situación para desesperarse
pero ¿quién me desesperó a Julia de Burgos
cuando era todo poesía? ¿por qué no esperó
con su tea en la mano que era su río
dulce de Loíza para que no se lo salara el mar?

La Habana esperaba entonces a un niño extraño
que venía creciendo en el Colegio de Belén
¿por qué no lo esperó?

y a mí ¿por qué no me esperó?
¿a mí que venía con un inmenso racimo
de esperanzas y una inmensa canasta de ternura?

¡Qué de cosas hacen ustedes con la poesía!

¡Cómo les gusta ver a un gran poeta suicidándose!

Sí
a ustedes

de todos modos Julia de Burgos no
definitivamente no
y por lo más profundo de lo más sagrado
inquebrantablemente no

5

But
why did they make her leave naked
from the Río Grande de Loíza
and force her to start walking after love
around the corners of Havana?
Havana? Havana was then
a capitalist seaquake full of spectators
and we all sank facing the Malecón
Havana was a situation for losing hope
but who made my Julia de Burgos lose hope
when everything was poetry? why didn't she wait
with her torch in hand that was her sweet Loíza
so the sea wouldn't taint the river with salt?

Havana then was waiting for a strange boy
who was growing up at the Belén Prep School,
why didn't she wait for him?

and me, why didn't she wait for me?
for me who came with an immense cluster
of hopes and an immense basket of tenderness?

You readers make up so much about poetry!

How you like to see a great poet commit suicide!

Yes
to you all

nonetheless Julia de Burgos no
definitely no
and for the most profound of the most sacred
unswervingly no

6

Ahora no venga nadie a la Quinta Avenida
a mirarla dormida en su cuneta
ahora no venga nadie

dado que todas las puertas aletearon
como una bandada de cernícalos
ahora no venga nadie

apenas abrió la boca y se la atragantaron
de amores desgraciados
le arrebataron de las manos la tea
empujaron su río a desembocar en el mar
(«el mar y tú» de los grandes amores
y de los martirios personales que llamamos
amor y a veces agonía)
ahora no venga nadie

nadie
ahora no venga Julia de Burgos victimaria
a recoger las lágrimas de Julia de Burgos
su víctima
para hacer collares y adornarse con ellas

para morir de amores todas las tardes
antes de la verbena
junto a la ventana

ahora no venga nadie
ahora por favor que no venga nadie
nadie
y decididamente no
y no por las razones del inefable sí

6

Don't anyone come now to Fifth Avenue
to look at her sleeping in its gutter
don't anyone come now

given that all the doors flapped
like a cast of hawks
don't anyone come now

she barely opened her mouth and choked
on her unhappy loves
they grabbed the torch from her hands
they forced her river to empty into the sea
(*"the sea and you"** from the great loves
and great personal torments we call
love and sometimes anguish)
don't anyone come now

no one
murderer Julia de Burgos don't come now
to gather the tears of Julia de Burgos
your victim
for making necklaces and adorning yourself with them

for dying of loves every evening
before the verbena
next to the window

don't anyone come now
please don't anyone come now
nobody
and decidedly no
and not for reasons of the ineffable yes

---

* "the sea and you swim up to me, / and in the madness of loving me until the shipwreck / you both go smashing ports and oars." —Julia de Burgos, "The Sea and You"

sino por las razones del inconmovible no
por las razones cristalinas
y traspasadas por el sol del mediodía
del imperturbable porque no

but for reasons of the unshakable no
for reasons crystal-clear
and pierced by the midday sun
of the impassive because no

7

Ciertamente
>   a Julia de Burgos
>   que era la esperanza
>   la negó Julia de Burgos
>   que era la desesperación

pero ya vendrán las anchas navegaciones
por los anchos océanos

>   a Julia de Burgos
>   que era el día de mañana
>   la negó Julia de Burgos
>   que era la noche anterior

pero ya vendrán las anchas reverberaciones
sobre los anchos océanos

7

Of course
>	to Julia de Burgos
>	who was hope
>	she rejected Julia de Burgos
>	who was hopelessness

but soon the broad ships will come
by the broad oceans

>	to Julia de Burgos
>	who was tomorrow's day
>	she rejected Julia de Burgos
>	who was the night before

but soon the broad shocks will come
over the broad oceans

8

Por el estricto rostro de las avellanas
las aves llenas
las avenas finas

por el laberinto de las caracolas
las claras colas
y las islas caras

por el limpio espejo de las caravanas
las vanas caras
y las carabinas

8

By the strict face of filberts
full birds
fine-milled oats

by the labyrinth of seashells
shelled seas
and steep islands

by the clean mirror of caravans
vain faces
and carbines

9

Vendrán los días y las melodías
sobre los rompevientos y las hortalizas
mi prima Eloísa se quitará la ropa
y se hundirá desnuda en el Río Grande
de Loíza y Carolina su compañera
vendrá del cementerio conocido
con Julia de Burgos desencadenada

También el capellán de la Policía
y el encargado de los Pasaportes
le tomarán el brazo y su brazo libre
seguirá siendo libre
para que entonces en la plataforma
de los ferrocarriles salten de pronto
libres todos los brazos

¡Qué de cosas hacen ustedes con la poesía!

¡Cuánto les gusta ver a un poeta suicidándose!

9

Days and melodies will come
over the windbreaks and vegetable gardens
my cousin Eloísa will take off her clothes
and sink naked in the Rio Grande
de Loíza and her girlfriend Carolina
will come from the famous cemetery
with Julia de Burgos unchained

Likewise the police chaplain
and the passport officer
will take her by the arm and her free arm
will keep being free
so that on the train platform
all of a sudden
all arms will break free

You readers make up so much about poetry!

You really do like to see a poet commit suicide!

10

Vendrán las mariposas de las factorías
pero una vez más cuidado
cuidado con el cuidado

Julia de Burgos cuidado con el suicidio
la humanidad no se suicida

la humanidad es una enredadera

sólo trepa y se agarra a las paredes
muertas y las llena de flores sobrentendidas

Julia de Burgos cuidado con Julia de Burgos
América Latina cuidado con América Latina

lo demás es una sombra cualquiera
en el fondo del corazón
las sombras danzan una alegre contradanza
y una vez más volverá Julia de Burgos
a bailar con Julia de Burgos
la alegre contradanza de la vida

10

Butterflies will come from factories
but once again beware
beware with care

Julia de Burgos beware of suicide
humanity doesn't commit suicide

humanity is a climbing vine

it just climbs and clings to barren walls
and fills them with flowers we know so well

Julia de Burgos beware of Julia de Burgos
Latin America beware of Latin America

everything else is just any shadow
in the pit of the heart
shadows whirl doing a merry contradance
and Julia de Burgos will be back dancing
once again with Julia de Burgos
the merry contradance of life

Jonathan Cohen is an award-winning translator of Latin American poetry and scholar of inter-American literature. In addition to Pedro Mir, he has translated Ernesto Cardenal, Enrique Lihn, Homero Aridjis, Octavio Paz, Javier Heraud, and Roque Dalton, among others. He is the translator (with Donald D. Walsh) of Mir's *Countersong to Walt Whitman and Other Poems*, originally published in 1993 by Azul Editions and reissued in 2018 by Peepal Tree Press. For more information about Cohen's work, see jonathancohenweb.com.

Chiqui Vicioso is a prominent Dominican poet, playwright, essayist, journalist, and cultural activist. Her many books include *Cómo escribir un poema con Pedro Mir* (How to Write a Poem with Pedro Mir), written to commemorate the centenary of Mir's birth, and the biographical work, *Julia de Burgos: La nuestra* (Julia de Burgos: Ours). A graduate of Brooklyn College and Columbia University, she lived in the United States for sixteen years. In 1988 she returned to her homeland, where she currently lives in Santo Domingo.

Also from Spuyten Duyvil

PABLO NERUDA
GRAPES AND THE WIND

Translated by Michael Straus
Introductory Essay by Helene J. F. de Aguilar
Illustrations by Anna Pipes
Design by Practical People
ISBN 978-1-944682-98-9 pbk. 344 pages $18.00
ISBN 978-1-944682-99-6 hdc. $24.00

Despite being one of Neruda's most important works following publication of *Canto general*, *Las uvas y el viento* (1954; *Grapes and the Wind*) has never previously been translated into English. He wrote this book when in political exile from his Chile because of his membership in the Communist Party. Here, he describes a political and poetic landscape during post-WWII ranging from Isla Negra in Chile to Mao's China. In essence, the poem is Neruda's hymn to newly-emergent nations and societies in Europe and Asia while at the same time comprising a lyric to his distant homeland.

"**Like the landscape of his native Chile**, Neruda's poetry encompasses great extremes—peak and prairie, deluge and drought—all connected by a spine of unbreakable certainty. Those of us who lack the language in which Neruda traversed this demanding terrain will find in Michael Straus a sure-footed and resourceful guide. Attentive alike to the humble and the historic, Neruda's work, in this fine version, retains all its power to move, to hold, to shock and to inspire."
—Grahame Davies

"**Poems of travel the ultimate Neruda** is found within, blown from country to country: 'I went singing / wandering…' As if to wander is to sing, and the poetry this poet effected is in sum an ode to flux. Why not? The Po River sings to him. Why should he not sing in return? Bread and blood sing to him too: politics and daily life. Michael Straus' translations of these poems bring to light Neruda's identity as an ego obscured in the surrealism of plants, places, and people. Straus has found English that synchs with Neruda's desire. 'Prepare yourself / for peace…' With Straus' help, we can."
—Vincent Katz

"**Thanks to this translation of Neruda's** *Las uvas y el viento*, we English readers have been given a gift, this long song from a poet who loved our blue planet. This is his ode to its brilliant shimmer, foibled as it is. In his Whitmanesque way, this is a different exploration than Neruda's renowned love poems, as he takes us to each vineyard, steel mill, or sleeping city, in an almost reckless way. And with this offering our understanding of the poet's span of perspective, including those of his politics, is deepened, as existentially expressed in its epilogue of 'Yo he visto': he has seen, heard and given it back to us."
—Sophie Cabot Black

www.ingramcontent.com/pod-product-compliance
Lightning Source LLC
Chambersburg PA
CBHW010408130526
44592CB00050B/2651